Vegan Slow Coc
For Eating
and
Staying Lean

By Anita Thomas

As a thank you for purchasing, please accept this free gift by visiting the link below…

www.veganslowcookerrecipes.com

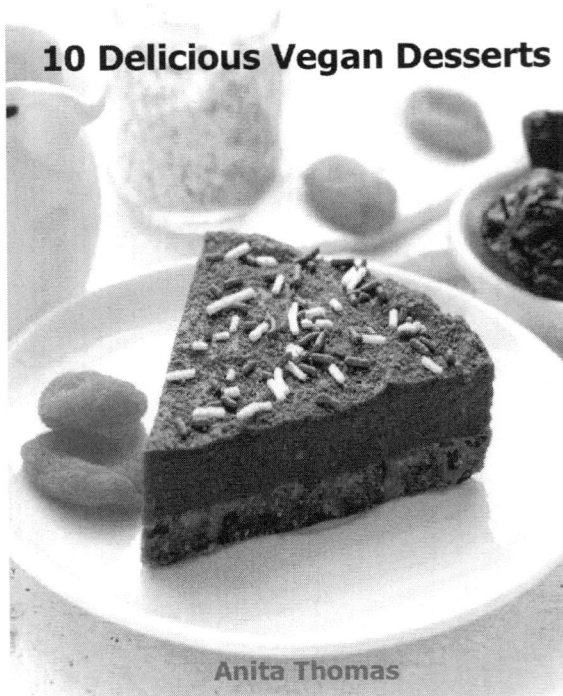

10 Delicious Vegan Desserts

Anita Thomas

DISCLAIMER

Hello and welcome to my book of vegan slow cooker recipes!

Inside *Vegan Slow Cooker Recipes for Eating Clean and Staying Lean* you'll find a variety of different slow cooker recipes, designed to make you feel clean from the inside, so that you stay lean on the outside.

Feel free to drop in and out of this book, using it to create mouthwatering vegan recipes that are simple to prepare and taste absolutely delicious. This book is designed as a quick and simple to follow guide you can use when you're stuck for time and want to create a tasty meal.

The recipes are listed by soups and stews, main courses and side dishes – but feel free to make them at any time during the day. You might even want to consider saving some in the slow cooker for breakfast if you're rushed for time.

Looking to lose weight? As all of the recipes inside this book are vegan and therefore plant based, they contain no animal products. So you'll find that all the recipes are naturally low in saturated fat, making it easier to keep the weight off when this lifestyle is followed long term.

There are many benefits to adopting a vegan lifestyle and this includes weight loss, lower cholesterol and blood pressure. You'll discover that you feel lighter after meals and as these slow cooker meals contain no dairy, all the food is hormone free and cruelty free, which benefits the body and mind greatly.

Some of the recipes in this book may surprise you. Sure there are lentil dishes and tofu based meals, but meat eaters will also find alternatives to many of their favorite foods such as beef in the Crock Pot BBQ 'Beef' recipe that uses seitan as a meat replacement (a form of wheat gluten), to mimic the taste.

Plus as all of the recipes can be set in the crockpot and left to cook, there's no reason why you can't leave it and come back hours later when the food is ready. That's why in the modern hectic schedule, crockpot cooking is so popular and why so many are looking for healthier options to feed them and their families.

Vegan crockpot cooking in particular can be inexpensive; especially when staples such as rice, beans, lentils, pulses and chopped tomatoes are bought in bulk. Tofu, seitan and soya can be used sparingly and are also good sources of protein.

I hope *Vegan Slow Cooker Recipes for Eating Clean and Staying Lean* will inspire you to live a healthier and more ethical lifestyle that will provide you with the steps necessary to feel better in the long term.

To your good health,

Anita Thomas

P.S: Please note that all nutritional serving information is for the entire batch, not per individual serving.

Table of Contents

Curried Vegetables and Chickpea Stew

This is a delicious stew that is simple to make and can be made with leftover vegetables and a can of chickpeas. It can be high in sodium however, so skip the salt if you wish.

Ingredients

1 teaspoon of olive oil
1 large diced onion
2 diced potatoes
1 tablespoon curry powder
1 tablespoon brown sugar
1 tablespoon salt
3 minced garlic cloves
1 inch piece of peeled and grated ginger
1 can diced of tomatoes with their juices
2 (16 ounce) cans of drained and rinsed chickpeas
1/8 teaspoon cayenne pepper
2 cups vegetable broth
1 diced green bell pepper
1 diced red bell pepper
1 cauliflower medium sized head cut into bite-sized florets
¼ teaspoon black pepper
10 ounces of baby spinach
1 cup coconut milk

Method

1. Into a skillet, heat the oil and add the onion, sautéing with the teaspoon of salt until it's then translucent, which should take about 5 minutes. Add in the potatoes along with a teaspoon of salt and sauté until the edges also become translucent.

2. Stir in the brown sugar, garlic, ginger, curry powder and the chili until the mixture becomes fragrant, which should take about 30 seconds. Pour in the ¼ cup of broth, making sure that you scrape the bottom of the pan to ensure it's deglazed.

3. Into the slow cooker, add the chickpeas, broth, cauliflower, bell pepper, tomatoes and their juices. Add in the pepper and the final teaspoon of salt. Make sure to stir well to combine all of the ingredients. The liquid should be halfway up to the sides of the bowl, and be sure to add in more broth if necessary.

4. Cover and then allow to cook in the slow cooker for 4 hours on a high heat. Stir in the spinach along with the coconut milk and cover the lid for 1 minute until the spinach starts to wilt. Taste and then adjust the salt as necessary, along with other seasonings. Serve with cous cous or on its own as desired.

Serves: 8-10
Calories (Total): 914kcal. Carbs: 146g 53%. Protein: 26g 24%, Fat: 25g 34%, Saturated Fat: 7.2g 29%, Cholesterol: 0mg, Sodium: 3,662 244%, Fiber: 26g 105%, Sugar: 35g 35%, Vitamin A: 2091IU, Vitamin C: 339mg, Calcium: 692mg 69%, Iron 9.1mg 51%, Potassium: 2,288 49%

These Indian spiced lentils make an excellent and comforting dish, especially when served with rice or quinoa.

Ingredients

2 cups of red lentils
10 ounces spinach
1 chopped onion
1 15 ounce can of diced tomatoes
1 tablespoon of minced garlic
1 tablespoon of minced fresh ginger
4 cups of vegetable broth
1 teaspoon mustard seeds
½ teaspoon ground cumin
1/8-1/4 teaspoon cayenne pepper
Juice of ½ a lemon or a lime
2 teaspoons sugar
1 ½ teaspoons kosher salt
1 teaspoon curry powder or paste
Handful of chopped cilantro

Method

1. Add all of the above ingredients into the slow cooker, except for the lemon or lime juice and the cilantro.
2. Cook on a high temperature for 3-4 hours, or for 6-7 hours on a low heat. Bring to the boil on the stove and then simmer while covered for 1 hour.
3. Before you serve the dish, add in the lemon juice and the cilantro. This is especially delicious when served with rice or quinoa, but you might want to consider naan bread or poppadoms instead.

Serves: 8
Calories (Total): 790kcal 36%. Carbs: 146g 53%. Protein: 49g 45%, Fat: 4.1g 6%, Saturated Fat: 0.5g 2%, Cholesterol: 0g 0%. Sodium: 3,539mg 236%. Fiber: 43g 172%. Sugar: 44g, 80%. Vitamin A: 29,484+ 590%. Vitamin C: 130mg 173%. Calcium: 532mg 53%. Iron: 26mg, 142%. Potassium: 3,277mg 70%.

This 'creamy' mushroom soup is a perfect winter warmer – without any added dairy.

Ingredients

2 tablespoons of extra virgin olive oil
1 diced yellow onion
2 diced garlic cloves
10 diced button mushrooms
6-8 sliced baby Portobello mushrooms
2 medium/large diced and peeled potatoes
¼ cup of white wine
4 cups of plain unsweetened soy milk
3 teaspoons of sweet white miso
Finely minced fresh parsley for garnishing

Method

1. In a large pot heat some oil and sauté the onions and garlic together for 2-3 minutes.
2. Stir in the mushrooms and the potatoes, sautéing for an extra 2-3 minutes.
3. Add the soy milk, wine, salt and pepper into the mixture. Cover and then bring to the boil. Reduce this heat to a low temperature and cook for one hour.
4. Once the soup has been heated, pour into a blender and blend until the mixture becomes creamy. Add back into the pot.
5. Add a small amount of the soup into a bowl and then stir in the miso, allowing it to dissolve. Cook over a low heat uncovered, for up to 3 to minutes.
6. Salt and pepper can be used for seasoning and fresh parsley can be used to garnish.

Serves: 4-5
Calories (Total): 1534kcal (383.5kcal a serving). Carbs: 216g 79%. Protein: 60g 54%. Fat: 51g 6.9%. Cholesterol: 0mg 0%. Sodium: 639mg 43%. Fiber: 26g 103%. Sugar: 54g 99%. Vitamin A: 5,102IU 102%. Vitamin C: 150mg 201%. Calcium: 476mg 48%. Iron: 15.4g 86%. Potassium: 4,477mg 95%.

This hearty soup is ideal for keeping you warm during winter.

Ingredients

2 tablespoons of olive oil
4 garlic cloves
1 medium yellow onion
1/2lb carrots
1lb dry navy beans
4 celery stalks
1 whole bay leaf
1 tsp dried rosemary
½ tsp dried thyme
½ tsp smoked paprika
Freshly cracked pepper

Method

1. Mince the onion, garlic, celery and slice the carrots. Add the olive oil, onion, garlic, carrots and the celery into a large slow cooker.
2. Give the beans a rinse and add them into the slow cooker along with thyme, rosemary, bay leaf, paprika and freshly cracked pepper.
3. Into the slow cooker add six cups of water, stirring and combining the ingredients. Place the lid on the top of the slow cooker and cook for 8 hours on a low setting.
4. After 8 hours, be sure to stir the soup and mash the beans a little. Add ½ a teaspoon of salt in as you desire. Ladle into bowls and serve with bread.

Serves: 6-8
Calories (Total): 708kcal 32%. Carbs: 92g 34%. Protein: 24g 22%. Fat: 30g 40%. Saturated Fat: 4.4g 18%. Cholesterol: 0mg. Sodium: 4,818mg 321%. Fiber: 25g 99%. Sugar: 24g 44%. Vitamin A: 768IU 15%. Vitamin C:80mg 106%. Calcium: 229mg 23%. Iron: 6.4mg 36%. Potassium: 2,532mg 54%.

This tasty stew is an exciting way to use butternut squash and red lentils together to create a meal that's both colorful and delicious.

Ingredients

1 chopped yellow onion
1 chopped large carrot
2 cloves of minced garlic
1 butternut squash, peeled and chopped
1 seeded and minced jalapeno
2-3 tsp garam masala
1 28oz can diced tomatoes in tomato juice
1 cup red lentils
2 15oz cans of drained and rinsed chickpeas
1-2 tsp sea salt
1 quart vegetable broth
1 tbsp olive or canola oil
Freshly minced cilantro for serving

Method

1. Into a large skillet add the oil over a medium high heat. Add in the carrot, onion and jalapeno, sautéing for six minutes. Add in the minced garlic for another 30 seconds and then add in the garam masala, stirring in the mixture and coating it well. Remove from the heat.
2. Place the onion mixture, butternut squash, chickpeas, red lentils, canned diced tomatoes and the vegetable broth into your slow cooker. Turn the heat on low and cook for an average of 8-10 hours. The longer this is cooked, the thicker the stew will be.
3. Add seasoning with sea salt to taste and then serve with the minced cilantro on top of the dish. This stew will freeze well and can be kept in the fridge for 5 days.

Serves: 4-6
Calories (Total): 1142kcal 115%. Carbs: 421g 153%. Protein: 138g 125%. Fat: 40g 55%. Saturated Fat: 40g 55%. Cholesterol: 0mg 0%. Sodium: 6,167mg 411%. Fiber: 110g 441%. Sugar: 83g 151%. Vitamin A: 5,649IU 113%. Vitamin C: 662mg 66%. Iron:47mg 261%. Potassium: 5,087mg 108%.

An exciting Asian soup that's full of spice and flavor, this recipe is easy to prepare and is excellent as a starter or on its own.

Ingredients
8oz extra firm tofu cut into small cubes
3 tbsp thai curry paste
1 tbsp canola oil
6 thai basil leaves (torn)
2 tsp brown sugar
½ tsp salt
1 14oz can coconut milk
2 cups vegetable broth
1 6-inch stalk lemongrass
½ a lime, juiced
2 red or green Thai chillies
½ cup dry jasmine rice
Cilantro (for garnishing)

Method

1. In a cup, cook the rice using a half a cup of water until the rice is tender. This should take about 30 minutes. Fluff the rice and then place aside.
2. Use a teaspoon of oil to heat a large nonstick skillet on a high heat. Add in the cubed tofu, curry paste, mashing them together in the oil until the mixture is well combined. Stir as you cook for another 2 minutes and then whisk it in slowly with the broth and the coconut milk.
3. After adding in the vegetable broth, add the brown sugar, salt, Thai basil, lemongrass stalk, lime juice and chilies, stirring for ten minutes. Place in the slow cooker and allow the flavors to develop for 1-2 hours.
4. Add in the cooked rice to individual bowls (or place in the slow cooker first with the liquid, depending on your preferences). Ladle the soup in and sprinkle with the chopped cilantro. Before serving the soup, remember to remove the chilies and lemongrass (you don't want to eat these).

Serves: 4
Calories (Total): 956kcal 43%. Carbs: 104g 38%. Protein: 25g 22%. Fat: 46g 63%. Fat: 46g 63%. Saturated Fat: 23g 95%. Cholesterol: 0mg 0%. Sodium: 3,103mg 207%. Fiber: 2g 8%. Sugar: 16.6g 30%. Vitamin A: 7,750IU 155%. Vitamin C: 4.1mg 5%. Calcium: 516mg 52%. Iron: 7.7mg, 43%. Potassium: 335mg 7%.

This soup will keep you feeling full and is an excellent idea for a meal when you're feeling lazy.

Ingredients

9 cups vegetable broth
6 cups of peeled, diced potatoes
1 large zucchini, quartered and thinly sliced
1 large sweet onion
3 cloves of garlic
1 tbsp extra virgin olive oil
½ tsp curry powder (optional)
Sea salt (to taste)
Freshly grated pepper (to taste)

Method

1. Add the vegetable broth into the large slow cooker. Peel and then dice the potatoes, adding those in.
2. Into a large skillet, add olive oil and heat to a medium-high temperature. As the skillet is heating up, chop the onions and quarter the zucchini, slicing thinly. Add this to the skillet, stirring occasionally.
3. Halfway through the cooking, add some garlic and then when the onions and zucchini are starting to become translucent, transfer this into the slow cooker.
4. Stir in the sea salt, pepper and curry powder. Allow to slow cook for 6-8 hours on a low temperature. In the last half hour of cooking, use the immersion blender for 15 seconds in one area. Stir this and then check for the appearance and taste.
5. For a thicker soup, repeat with the immersion blender. Cook for an extra 30 minutes. Serve the soup with some lovely gluten free bread.

Serves: 4
Calories (Total): 1112kcal 51%. Carbohydrates: 226g, 82%. Protein: 18.9g, 17%. Fat: 15g 20%. Saturated Fat: 2.2g 9%. Cholesterol: 0mg 0%. Sodium: 8,603mg 574%. Fiber: 19.1g 76%. Sugar: 34g 61%. Vitamin A: 4,606IU, 92%. Vitamin C: 133mg, 178%. Calcium: 70mg 7%. Iron: 3mg 17%. Potassium: 3,791mg 81%.

This soup is a perfect winter warmer and is also high in Vitamin A and potassium.

Ingredients

2 large parsnips, peeled and chopped
1 large yellow onion, chopped
1 fuji apple, peeled and chopped
1 small butternut squash, peeled, seeds and chopped into small squares (about 5 cups)
2 cups low sodium vegetable broth
1/8 teaspoon ground sage
½ teaspoon ground cumin
¼ teaspoon dried thyme
½ teaspoon ground coriander
½ teaspoon salt

Method:

1. Add all of the above ingredients into a crock pot and cook on a low temperature for 6 hours.
2. After the vegetables are cooked, add the soup to a blender and blend the mixture until smooth.

Serves: 4-6 people
Calories (Total): 585kcal 27%. Carbohydrates: 144g 52%. Protein: 9g 8%. Fat: 0.7g 1%. Saturated Fat: 0.2g 1%. Cholesterol: 0mg 0%. Sodium: 328mg 22%. Fiber: 29g 116%. Sugar: 44g 81%. Vitamin A: 74,510+ 1490+. Vitamin C: 195mg 44%. Calcium: 436mg 44%. Iron: 6.7mg 37%. Potassium: 3,224mg 69%.

This tasty African stew is high in Vitamin A and a good source of carbohydrates and protein, meaning it will keep you feeling fuller for longer.

Ingredients

2 medium sized sweet potatoes, peeled and then chopped into bite-sized pieces
1 large sweet onion, chopped
1 large red bell pepper, or 2 small ones, chopped
2 heaped tablespoons peanut butter
¼ cup dark brown sugar
¾ teaspoon salt
1 (14.5 ounce) can lite coconut milk
1 (15-19 ounces) can garbanzo beans, rinsed and drained
1 14.5 ounce can of diced tomatoes
2 inches of fresh ginger, peeled
1 teaspoon ground cumin
½ teaspoon ground cinnamon
¼ teaspoon ground red pepper (cayenne)
1 tablespoon curry powder
3-4 garlic cloves
1 cup loosely packed fresh cilantro leaves and stems

Method:
1. Into a food processor add the garlic cloves, cilantro, ginger, tomatoes, cumin, cinnamon, peanut butter, curry powder and ground red pepper. Blend this until the mixture is pureed and looks thick and pasty.
2. Into the slow cooker add the chopped onions, red bell peppers, garbanzo beans and the sweet potatoes. Add in the brown sugar, coconut milk, peanut sauce mixture, stirring to gently mix all of the ingredients together.
3. Turn the slow cooker on to a low temperature and then cook for 6-8 hours. Serve the stew with rice and top with some sliced green onions and fresh cilantro.

Serves: 4-6
Calories (Total): 1525kcal 69%. Carbohydrates: 266g 97%. Protein: 45g 41%. Fat: 43g 58%. Saturated Fat: 23g 92%. Cholesterol: 0mg 0%. Sodium: 2,495mg 166%. Fiber: 42g 168%. Sugar: 99g 180%. Vitamin A: 45,803+ 916%. Vitamin C: 297mg 396%. Calcium: 377mg 38%. Iron: 15.6mg 87%. Potassium: 2,256mg 48%.

The ideal soup to make on a rainy day, curled up on the sofa and watching the world pass by. This healthy soup is rich in protein, Vitamin A, iron and potassium.

Ingredients

2 cloves minced garlic
1 sweet onion, diced
1 medium sweet potato, peeled and cut into 1" cubes
2 celery stalks, diced
2 carrots, peeled and sliced into 1" pieces
1 cup whole kernel corn
1 bay leaf
1 teaspoon paprika
1/8 teaspoon allspice
½ teaspoon black pepper
Kosher or sea salt (to taste)
½ teaspoon crushed red pepper flakes
4 cups low sodium vegetable broth
2 cups fresh or frozen green beans
1 (14.5 oz) can diced tomatoes
2 cans cannellini beans, drained and rinsed

Method:

1. Place all of the above ingredients into a slow cooker, stirring to ensure they are thoroughly combined. Cover and then cook for 8-10 hours on a low temperature, until the carrots become tender.
2. Serve with warm crusty bread and enjoy!

Serves: 6
Calories: (Total) 880kcal 40%. Carbohydrates: 180g 65%. Protein: 23g 21%. Fat: 3g 4%. Saturated Fat: 0.2g 1%. Cholesterol: 0.2mg 0%. Sodium: 2,583mg 172%. Fiber: 50g 200%. Sugar: 89g 143%. Vitamin A: 50,425+IU. Vitamin C: 193mg 257%. Calcium: 413mg 41%. Iron: 13.2mg 72%. Potassium: 3,813mg 81%.

Lentil Chili

A simple yet comforting dish that's perfect for any weather.

Ingredients

1 tablespoon of olive oil
2 medium chopped onions
6-8 minced garlic cloves
2 chopped carrots
1 chopped celery stalk
2 tablespoons chili powder
2 teaspoons cumin powder
1 teaspoon coriander powder
1 teaspoon dry mustard
1 teaspoon dried oregano
One 28 ounce box of crushed tomatoes
One 16 ounce package dry lentils
6-7 cups of vegetable broth
Salt to taste

Method

1. Into a large pot, heat some oil. Add in the garlic, onions, celery and carrot. Sauté the onions until they are lightly browned and soft, which should take about 3-4 minutes.
2. Add in the cumin, chili powder, oregano, coriander and mustard, stirring well for 1-2 minutes. Add in the tomatoes plus the salt to taste. Pour this mixture into the crockpot and then add in the lentils and the 6 cups of vegetable broth.
3. Cook for 4-6 hours, adding more water in as needed so you can achieve the desired consistency.

Serves: 12
Calories: (Total) 1222kcal 152%. Carbohydrates: 620g 225%. Protein: 109g 99%. Fat: 21g 29%. Saturated Fat: 2.9g 12%. Cholesterol: 0mg 0%. Sodium: 80,135+IU 5342%. Fiber: 139g 410%. Sugar: 226g 410%. Vitamin A: 44,867+IU 897%. Vitamin C: 125mg 167%. Calcium: 328mg 33%. Iron: 50mg 280%. Potassium: 1,004mg 21%.

This Caribbean dish takes some preparation, but is well worth it after a long day at the office. You can swap the vegetable bouillon for vegan based 'Not Chick'n' or 'Not Beef' bouillons instead for a more authentic flavor.

Ingredients

1 ½ cup of chopped bell pepper
3 minced garlic cloves
8 ounces of tempeh, cut into bite-sized pieces
1 ½ cups of diced tomatoes
1 teaspoon of vegetable bouillon
1-2 teaspoons Cajun seasoning
¼ to ½ teaspoon of liquid smoke or smoked paprika
3 cups water
¾ cup of quinoa, rinsed well
Tabasco sauce or hot pepper (optional)
Salt and pepper (to taste)

Method:

1. The night before you prepare this dish, place the tempeh and the vegetables in the fridge.
2. In the morning, add the chopped bell pepper, garlic cloves, tempeh, diced tomatoes, vegetable bouillon, Cajun seasoning, smoked paprika and the water into the oiled slow cooker. Cook these ingredients on a low heat for 6-19 hours.
3. Around 1-2 hours before serving, ensure that the slow cooker is turned on high and add in the quinoa. Cook this until the quinoa starts to form white rings – that's when they're ready. Taste to ensure you are satisfied and then add in the Tabasco sauce, cayenne pepper and the salt if desired.

Serves: 4
Calories: (Total): 1072kcal 49%. Carbohydrates: 138g 50%. Protein: 64g 58%. Fat: 32g 43%. Saturated Fat: 5g 20%. Cholesterol: 0mg 0%. Sodium: 1047mg 70%. Fiber: 35g 138%. Sugar: 14.3g 26%. Vitamin A: 1624IU 32%. Vitamin C: 315mg 420%. Calcium: 280mg 28%. Iron: 15.3mg 85%. Potassium: 1597mg 34%.

This delicious chili is easy to prepare and can then be left in the slow cooker for hours while you go about your day.

Ingredients

1 diced onion
1 red or yellow bell pepper (chopped)
2 carrots (grated or thinly sliced)
1 zucchini (diced)
2 cloves of minced garlic
2 cans of kidney beans
1 ½ cup corn
1 ½ tbsp chili powder
1 tsp cumin
2 15 ounce cans diced tomatoes
½ tsp red pepper flakes
A dash of cayenne pepper
A dash of Tabasco sauce (optional)

Method:

1. Take all of the above ingredients and place them into the slow cooker.
2. Cover the slow cooker and cook on a low heat for an average of 6-8 hours.

Serves: 5
Calories: (Total) 887kcal 40%. Carbohydrates: 171g 62%. Protein: 46g 42%. Fat: 5.2g 7%. Saturated Fat: 1.1g 5%. Cholesterol: 0mg 0%. Sodium: 2,537mg 169%. Fiber: 48g 193%. Sugar: 47g 86%. Vitamin A: 3,950IU 79%. Vitamin C: 378mg 505%. Calcium: 351mg 35%. Iron: 17.7mg 98%. Potassium: 4,506mg 96%.

A colorful and nutritious meal, the root veggies are an excellent source of vitamins and minerals.

Ingredients

2 cups (475ml) of water
½ cup of diced carrots
½ cup diced turnips or peeled rutabagas
½ cup (67g) of diced sweet potatoes or winter squash
2 minced garlic cloves
½ teaspoon dried oregano
½ teaspoon dried sage

1 cup (56g) minced greens like turnips, collards, kale, etc
½ teaspoon lemon zest
Salt and pepper (to taste

Method:

1. Add in all of the ingredients up to the minced greens, into the slow cooker. Cook on a low heat for 7-9 hours.
2. Around 30 minutes before the meal has to be served, add in the minced greens and the lemon zest. Add salt and pepper to taste just before serving and feel free to add in more sage and oregano if necessary.

Serves: 3
Calories (Total): 188 calories 9%. Carbohydrates: 42g 15%. Protein: 4.7g 4%. Fat: 1.1g 2% Saturated Fat: 0.4g 2%. Cholesterol: 0mg 0% Sodium: 650mg 43% Dietary Fiber: 10.2mg 41% Sugar: 18.4g 33% Vitamin A: 20,296+IU, 406% Vitamin C: 72mg 96% Calcium: 80mg 8% Iron: 3mg 17% Potassium: 1154mg 25%.

Just because you're vegan doesn't mean you have to miss out on BBQ! This tasty alternative will please even the pickiest of meat eaters.

Ingredients

8oz fresh seitan
½ batch Homemade BBQ sauce (see ingredients below for how to prepare)
or 1 bottle barbeque sauce
1 teaspoon garlic powder
1 teaspoon onion powder
Salt and pepper to taste
Wholemeal buns to serve (optional)
Salad to serve (optional)

Method:

1. Place the seitan, garlic and onion powder into the slow cooker, seasoning with salt and pepper.
2. Pour the barbeque sauce over the seitan. This should be cooked for 5-6 hours on a low temperature.
3. Remove the seitan from the slow cooker, shred and then return to the slow cooker for another 30 mins to 1 hour.

Homemade BBQ Sauce

Makes 2 cups

1 tbsp olive oil
2 cups ketchup
½ cup molasses
¼ cup diced white onion
2 tsp apple cider vinegar
1 tbsp liquid smoke
¼ cup vegan Worcestershire sauce
A pinch of cayenne

Method:

1. Heat oil in a medium sized pan. Add in the diced onions and sauté until the mixture becomes translucent. Let this cool. In the meantime add all the ingredients into a food processor or a blender, pureeing until smooth. Store this mixture in the refrigerator.

Serves: 8
Calories: (Total): 835kcal 38%. Carbohydrates: 118g 43%. Protein: 53g 48%. Fat: 19g 26%. Saturated Fat: 2g 8%. Cholesterol: 0mg 0%. Sodium: 2,792mg 186%. Fiber: 2.8mg 11%. Sugar: 95g 172%. Vitamin A: 0IU 0%.

Vitamin C: 2mg 3%. Calcium: 745mg 74%. Iron: 17.6mg 98%. Potassium: 1,994mg 42%.

Quinoa is an excellent source of proteins and essential amino acids. When combined with fresh green beans, carrots and sweet peppers it makes a delicious and highly nutritious meal.

Ingredients

1 small onion, chopped
1 tablespoon of olive oil
1 medium sweet red pepper, chopped
1 small carrot, chopped
1 cup fresh green beans, chopped
2 garlic cloves, minced
1 ½ cups quinoa
3 cups vegetable stock
1 teaspoon fresh cilantro or basil
¼ teaspoon black pepper

Method:

1. Rinse the quinoa thoroughly and then place it in the crock pot. Add the tablespoon of olive oil to coat the quinoa.
2. Stir in the vegetable broth, pepper, garlic and vegetables. Reserve the cilantro for later.
3. Cover the crock pot and cook for 4-6 hours on a low heat, or for 2-4 hours on a high heat.
4. Once the quinoa is done, fluff it using a fork and it should be tender. All of the liquid will have been absorbed into the quinoa.
5. Top the quinoa with fresh cilantro before serving.
6. Mix in the garbanzo or black beans to this dish. Serve and enjoy!

Serves: 4
Calories: (Total): 1264kcal 57%. Carbohydrates: 210g 76%. Protein: 42g 38%. Fat: 30g 41%. Saturated Fat: 3.9g 16%. Cholesterol: 0mg 0%. Sodium: 3,024mg 202%. Fiber: 29mg 49%. Sugar: 27g 49%. Vitamin A: 6142IU 123%. Vitamin C: 193mg 257%. Calcium: 223mg 22%. Iron: 13.7mg 76%. Potassium: 2,149mg 46%.

These crock pot tacos are delicious alternatives on a Mexican favorite. Enjoy!

Ingredients

1 onion, minced
1 tsp chili powder
1 tsp garlic powder
2 tsp cumin powder
1 tsp oregano
12 taco shells
2 cans (15oz) black beans
8oz can chopped green chilies
Your favorite toppings (e.g. tomatoes, jalapenos, vegan cheese, etc)

Method
1. Use a little nonstick spray in the slow cooker. Add all of the above ingredients, mixing well.
2. Cook on a low temperature for 6-8 hours, or a high of 3-5 hours.
3. Once the beans are cooked to the desired level, divide them between the eight taco shells.
4. Top with your favorite toppings and serve!

Serves: 6
Calories: (Total): 838kcal 38%. Carbohydrates: 151g 55%. Protein: 32g 29%. Fat: 20g 28%. Saturated Fat: 4g 16%. Cholesterol: 0mg 0%. Sodium: 2,939mg 196%. Fiber: 28mg 112%. Sugar: 17.8g 32%. Vitamin A: 726IU 15%. Vitamin C: 23mg 31%. Calcium: 333mg 33%. Iron: 10.8mg 60%. Potassium: 1630mg 35%.

A filling bowl of brown rice is a good source of protein and magnesium. It's made all the tastier with the beans, fresh vegetables and chilies for an extra spicy kick.

Ingredients

1 cup of long grain brown rice
2 cups of vegetable stock
1 cup finely chopped onion
1 red bell pepper
1 green bell pepper
4 ozs green chilies
15 ozs black beans
½ cup diced tomato
1 poblano pepper
½ a cup of thinly sliced green onion
½ cup freshly chopped cilantro
1 avocado
3 tbsps fresh lime juice
2 tbsps extra virgin olive oil
½ tsp ground cumin
Salt (to taste)

Method:

1. Place the rice, vegetable stock and the chopped onion into the slow cooker for one and a half hours until the rice is tenderized. As the rice is cooking, chop the red bell pepper and green pepper, opening the diced green chilies. Drain the black beans into a colander in the sink and rinse with the cold water until no foam appears. Allow the beans to drain.
2. After an hour and a half, add in the red bell pepper, green peppers and chilies with the juice. Add in the drained black beans to the slow cooker and combine with the rice. Add salt for taste and allow to cook for 30 minutes on a high temperature.
3. When the rice mixture has finished cooking, chop in the tomato, cilantro and the thinly sliced green onion, along with the poblano pepper. Cut the avocado into 1 inch cubes across and toss this into a bowl with the fresh lime juice. Use the bowl to store all of the salsa ingredients. Make sure to add in the tomato, chopped cilantro, poblano, cumin, green onion, 3 tablespoons of lime juice, salt and the olive oil, combining to taste.
4. When the rice is tender, that is when the slow cooker mixture is ready. The vegan brown rice Mexican bowl can be served either hot or cold and is particularly delicious with homemade salsa.

Serves: 6
Calories (Total): 1,699kcal 77%. Carbohydrates: 256g 93%. Protein: 45g 41%. Fat: 64g 87%. Saturated Fat: 13g 53%. Cholesterol: 0mg 0%. Sodium: 3211mg 214%. Fiber: 63mg 250%. Sugar: 28g 51%. Vitamin A: 1911IU

38%. Vitamin C: 351mg 468%. Calcium: 183mg 18%. Iron: 12.5mg 69%. Potassium: 3211mg 68%.

This recipe is high in carbohydrates and protein, essential for fueling the body. It is also low in cholesterol, making it a healthier alternative to its meat equivalent.

Ingredients

Polenta:
1 cup polenta
1 tbsp margarine
4 cups water

Method:

1. Take a baking sheet and cover with parchment paper. Set it aside and bring 4 cups of water to the boil. Slowly add in the polenta. Add margarine, stirring until it's of a thick consistency.
2. Pour the polenta onto the prepared baking sheet, spreading evenly so it's ¼ inch thick. Set this aside to cool. Once this is cool, cut the polenta into rectangles.

Lasagna:
A dash of olive oil
½ bunch of kale, washed and chopped
1 large Portobello mushroom, cut into 1 inch slices
4 cloves of minced garlic
½ large onion, finely chopped
1 tsp dried basil
1-2 cups marinara sauce
'Cheese' sauce
Sea salt and pepper

Method:

1. Heat 1-2 tbsps of olive oil into a large skillet over a medium heat. Add in the onions and mushrooms, sautéing until juicy. Add the garlic in and cook for another 1-2 minutes.
2. Add the kale, cooking until it's a bright green color and soft. Add the 'cheese' sauce in and cook until this has thickened and is no longer runny. Remove this from the heat, seasoning with salt and pepper if desired.
3. Use the marinara sauce to coat the bottom of the crockpot. Cover with the marinara sauce and a single layer of polenta slices. Place the kale mixture on top and repeat this in layers: marinara sauce, polenta, kale; then finish with another layer of polenta then marinara.
4. Cover the crockpot and cook on a high temperature for 3-4 hours. Uncover this and leave to set aside for 30 minutes before serving onto plates.

'Cheese' Sauce

Ingredients

1/3 cup raw cashews
¼ cup nutritional yeast
1 cup unsweetened non-dairy milk
1 tbsp lemon juice
2 tsp Dijon mustard
½ tsp onion powder
½ tsp garlic powder
2 tsp corn starch or arrowroot
½ tsp white pepper

1. Place all of the above ingredients into a blender and pulse blend until smooth.

Serves: 2- 3
Calories (Total): 1092kcal 50%. Carbohydrates: 175g 64%. Protein: 27g 24%. Fat: 33g 44%. Saturated Fat: 7.6g 31%. Cholesterol: 0mg 0%. Sodium: 2,565mg 171%. Fiber: 15.9g 64%. Sugar: 24g 44%. Vitamin A: 20,438+IU 409%. Vitamin C: 68mg 90%. Calcium: 644mg 64%. Iron: 5.1mg 28%. Potassium: 430mg 9%.

A simple and 'skinny' alternative to traditional spaghetti Bolognese. Feel free to use meat-free vegan mince if necessary.

Ingredients

1 tablespoon extra virgin olive oil
1 small sweet onion, diced
2 cloves minced garlic
3 teaspoons capers, drained
2 teaspoons dried oregano
¼ teaspoon red pepper flakes
½ teaspoon black pepper
2 (14.5 ounce) cans fire roasted tomatoes
8 ounces whole wheat spaghetti, broken into small pieces
1 cup arugula

Method:

1. Add the oil into a small skillet and sauté the onion over a medium-low heat until tender which will take about 4 minutes.
2. Add in the garlic and sauté for an extra minute. Into a large bowl combine the sautéed onion and the garlic, along with the remaining ingredients, except for the arugula.
3. Toss all of the ingredients well and ensure that the spaghetti is coated with sauce, before adding into the slow cooker.
4. Cover the slow cooker and then place on a low heat for 2-3 hours until the pasta is al dente. Add in the arugula for the last 10 minutes of cooking, stirring to ensure it's well combined.
5. Serve onto a platter and sprinkle with vegan cheese if desired.

Serves: 4
Calories (Total): 565kcal 26%. Carbohydrates: 95g 35%. Protein:17.9mg 16%. Fat: 15.5g 21%. Saturated Fat: 2.3g 9%. Cholesterol: 0mg 0% Sodium: 1,797mg 120%. Fiber: 21g 85%. Sugar: 25g 46%. Vitamin A:2,268IU 45%. Vitamin C:48mg 64%. Calcium: 186mg 19% Iron: 5mg 28%. Potassium:184mg 4%.

Side Dishes

Slow Cooker Potatoes with Garlic and Rosemary

A 5-7 quart slow cooker is recommended for this particular recipe.

Ingredients

¼ cup extra virgin olive oil
3 cloves minced garlic
1 tablespoon chopped fresh rosemary
4 medium sized red potatoes, cubed into ½" pieces
½ teaspoon black pepper
Kosher or sea salt to taste

Method:

1. Into the slow cooker, add oil and turn to a high heat as you prepare the potatoes. Around 15 minutes of preheating is good.
2. Combine all of the above ingredients into the slow cooker, tossing the potatoes with oil, and then covering and cooking on a high heat for 2-3 hours (4-5 hours on low) until the potatoes become brown and tender.

Serves: 6
Calories (Total): 736kcal. Carbohydrates: 136g 49%. Protein: 15.9g 14%. Fat: 15g 20%. Saturated Fat: 2.2g 9%. Cholesterol: 0mg 0%. Sodium: 188mg 13%. Fiber: 12.5g 50%. Sugar: 9.9g 18%. Vitamin A: 69iu 1%. Vitamin C: 87mg 116%. Calcium: 62mg 6%. Iron: 4.8mg 27%. Potassium: 3,771mg 80%.

A colorful side dish you can make in the slow cooker, perfect as an accompaniment to a roast dinner or Mediterranean dishes.

Ingredients

2-15oz cans fried apples
12 oz diced butternut squash

Method:
1. Use some cooking oil spray inside the slow cooker.
2. Place the butternut squash and the fried apples into the slow cooker and stir.
3. Cook on a low setting for 4 hours.

Serves: 6
Calories (Total): 1294kcal. Carbohydrates: 319g 116%. Protein: 3g 3%. Fat: 0.3g 0%. Saturated Fat: 0g 0%. Cholesterol: 0mg 0%. Sodium: 78mg 5%. Fiber: 24g 95%. Sugar: 257g 468%. Vitamin A: 758IU 15%. Vitamin C: 86mg 115%. Calcium: 13.3mg 1%. Iron: 11.6mg 64%. Potassium: 966mg 21%.

This is a good way to get greens into your diet. Collard greens are high in Vitamins A and C.

Ingredients

4 large bunches of collard greens (8 cups)
1 medium peeled white onion, diced
1 tablespoon raw apple cider vinegar
2 teaspoons coconut sugar
1 tablespoon extra virgin olive oil
4 peeled garlic cloves, minced
1 small dried chipotle chili pepper with the seeds and stems removed/diced
4 cups vegetable stock
2 tablespoons white wine

Method:

1. Prepare the collards for cooking. Remove the large ribs from the greens and stack the 4 or 5 leaves on top of one another, rolling them into a tight cylinder. Slice them lengthwise into large ribbons. Make sure to place the cut greens into a clean and sterilized sink that's filled with cold water, along with 1 teaspoon of sea salt, cleaning them thoroughly. This can take a few changes of water to clean thoroughly.
2. Transfer the greens into a strainer or a salad spinner, allowing them to drain free of water.
3. Heat a tablespoon of olive oil into the large pot, over a medium heat. Add in the chipotle pepper, onions and the minced garlic. Cook this for 2 minutes, stirring it frequently so that all of the vegetables don't burn.
4. Add in the green collards, sprinkling them with apple cider vinegar along with a sweetener of your choice, black pepper and sea salt to taste.
5. Add in the vegetable stock and the wine to the slow cooker, covering and cooking for 45-60 minutes until the vegetables become tender. Taste and then adjust the seasoning if desired.

Serves: 4-6
Calories (Total): 662kcal 30%. Carbohydrates: 104g 38%. Protein: 33g 30%. Fat: 19.5g 27%. Saturated Fat: 2.7g 11%. Cholesterol: 0mg 0%. Sodium: 7732mg 515%. Fiber: 44g 174%. Sugar: 26g 46%. Vitamin A: 102,000+IU 2040%. Vitamin C: 283mg 377%. Calcium: 2150mg 215%. Iron: 17.7mg 98%. Potassium: 1800mg 38%.

Slow cooked baked beans develop a distinct flavor and make the perfect side dish to any veggie burger.

Ingredients

1 medium yellow onion, diced
1 pound dried navy or pea beans
2½ cups water, plus more for soaking the beans
½ cup ketchup
¼ cup packed dark brown sugar
1 tablespoon Dijon mustard
¼ cup dark molasses
1 tablespoon kosher salt
1/8 teaspoon ground cloves
½ teaspoon freshly ground black pepper

Method:

1. Into a large bowl place the beans and pick through them, discarding any beans or stones as necessary. Cover the beans with at least 3 inches of cold water and allow to soak uncovered at a room temperature for about 8 hours overnight.
2. Drain in a colander and then reserve the bowl, setting it aside. Place the beans and the onion into the slow cooker.
3. Whisk in the remaining ingredients from the reserved bowl, until they are both well combined. Pour this into the slow cooker, stirring thoroughly until the mixture is well covered.
4. Cover in the slow cooker and cook on either high or a low heat until the beans become tender and the liquid has thickened slightly. EGANThis can take about 6 hours. Taste and then season with salt and pepper if desired.

Serves: 8-10
Calories (Total): 996kcal 45%. Carbohydrates: 212g 77%. Protein: 40g 37%. Fat: 3.2g 4%. Saturated Fat: 0.5g 2%. Cholesterol: 0g 0%. Sodium: 3662mg 244%. Fiber: 49g 196%. Sugar: 88g 160%. Vitamin A: 1120mg 22%. Vitamin C: 28mg 38%. Calcium: 355mg 35%. Iron: 11.3mg 63%. Potassium: 2223mg 47%.

This broccoli side dish has a distinctive nutty taste and is a good accompaniment to a variety of Asian dishes.

Ingredients

2 pounds broccoli florets
1 cup large raw hazelnuts
1 head garlic, peeled (12 cloves)
2 lemons, juiced
2 tablespoons olive oil
½ teaspoon kosher salt
½ teaspoon pepper

Method:
1. A 4 quart crockpot should be used for best results. First, wash and trim the broccoli, then add it to the crockpot. Peel the garlic and add in the salt and pepper. Add in the hazelnuts, squeezing in the lemon juice over the top. Toss together using wooden spoons.
2. Cover the crockpot and cook on a high heat for 2 hours, or for 4 hours on a low heat. The cooking is finished once the broccoli has reached the desired level of tenderness.

Serves: 2
Calories (Total): 775kcal 35%. Carbohydrates: 50g 18%. Protein: 26g 23%. Fat: 47g 64%. Saturated Fat: 5.8g 24%. Cholesterol: 0mg 0%. Sodium: 647mg 43%. Fiber: 25g 101%. Sugar: 24g 43%. Vitamin A: 211IU 4%. Vitamin C: 565mg 753%. Calcium: 68mg 7%. Iron: 1.1mg 6%. Potassium: 11mg 2%.

Thank you so much for reading my book and I hope you liked reading it. If you enjoyed it, I would appreciate if you could leave me a review on Amazon.

16063287R00023

Printed in Great Britain
by Amazon